D1027394

The
Profitable Power
of Purpose

7 Strategies for turning your
vision into a force for greater
passion, performance and profitability

Ian Percy

Inspired Productions Press, LLC
Scottsdale, Arizona

The Profitable Power of Purpose

Ian Percy

Printed in the United States of America

Cover design and layout by Booty Design and
Georgia Percy,
Scottsdale Arizona

Photography by Doug Crouch, Phoenix, Arizona

ISBN 0 9707140-9-2

Table of contents

Got Purpose? 7

Strategy 1: A Peak Purpose is Ecological! 19

Strategy 2: Let Your Irritations Inspire You! 29

Strategy 3: Allow Your Purpose to be
Awesome! 43

Strategy 4: Reflect the Perspective of the
Customer or Client! 49

Strategy 5: Express Your Passion! 57

Strategy 6: Keep the Purpose Flag Flying
High! 67

Strategy 7: It Unites and Energizes the
Organization Into Action! 77

The Strategies Summarized 85

20 Wicked Questions! 87

About Ian Percy 91

Other Purpose-full Resources! 93

The Profitable Power of Purpose

The Profitable Power of Purpose!

Got Purpose?

Most of the stuff we bandy about as a "mission" or "vision" is superficial mush.

The only way to fix that problem is to arouse energetic and insightful discussion about purpose throughout your organization. That is the purpose of this book. I chose to be content more with trying to create a hunger for the answers rather than exhaust the answers themselves.

No matter what you are trying to do, establishing a clear purpose is such a totally obvious first step it's almost embarrassing to mention it.

And that is precisely why any suggestion that

you'd ever become extremely busy in your work and personal life *without* a clearly defined purpose is likely to arouse a lot of defensiveness. It sure would for me. But that is exactly the situation for corporations, organizations and individuals all over the world.

As a desperate leader once declared, "Having lost sight of our objectives, let us redouble our efforts!" That is the mantra of far too many organizations today.

Imagine you and your organization getting back every dollar, hour and kilowatt of energy spent on pointless and non-productive activities. You'd add twenty years onto your life and have one happy bunch of shareholders, that's for sure.

And why did you get involved in those draining activities in the first place? I suggest in most cases it was an inadequately defined purpose.

It is no different on a personal level. You're holding down a demanding job; you coach soccer Saturdays; you sing in the choir on Sundays – and of course there's practice on Thursday evenings; you take turns taking one of your kids to dance class on Tuesdays after school; you're on three community agency boards, your spouse is trying to get a home-based network marketing business going so you can "have some time together;" the kids want a dog and on and on it goes. What exactly are you trying to do?

And stop going to seminars on life balance. There's no such thing. The only way you're going to get balanced is if you're dead. What we all need to do is get clear about life *purpose*. Things that are balanced don't move and they're boring. Life is meant for teetering and tottering!

Yet frenetic, pointless busy-ness is *the* bankrupting scourge in our businesses today. Sit down and count how many initiatives or projects are currently underway in your organization right now. It is not uncommon to list 20 or 30 of them even in a relatively small company. Do they all make sense to you? Are they all integrated and leading some-where? How many committees are there in the organization? What would happen if they never met again? Why exactly is your company moving its headquarters or heading into a merger? For what percentage of your day are you doing meaningful and worthwhile work that truly matters?

Questions like these can send a lot of organizations scrambling. In some instances the answers can be downright embarrassing.

Without question the senior executive team is the "Keeper of the Purpose." They are the ones who sharpen its definition and carry its flag. So it is reasonable to test for the presence of a higher purpose within executive ranks before doing anything else.

To get the conversation going, here are simple (though somewhat loaded) questions you can fill in and discuss at your next executive meeting.

- To what degree is our Executive Team totally unified and inspired by a common vision for where this company is heading?

1	2	3	4	5	6	7
Low						High

- How confident am I that a contagious passion for that vision has spread throughout our organization?

1	2	3	4	5	6	7
Low						High

- How confident am I that there is obvious synergy between all of our projects (technology, sales, operational restructuring, etc.) due to a grand and energizing overarching corporate vision?

1	2	3	4	5	6	7
Low						High

- How confident am I that each initiative, within itself, is driven by a crystal clear purpose?

1	2	3	4	5	6	7
Low						High

- How sure am I that all the people involved in these initiatives know, agree on and are enthused by what that purpose is?

1	2	3	4	5	6	7
Low						High

- How clear is it that each initiative will produce an ROI that will definitely make us glad we spent the time, energy and money on it?

1	2	3	4	5	6	7
Low						High

And then perhaps the most intimate and difficult question of them all…

- Have you ever driven to work asking yourself: "Why am I doing this?"

1	2	3	4	5	6	7
Low						High

This last question – which at first seems almost out of place – hints at the fact that, particularly on leadership levels, there needs to be a direct connection between one's life purpose and the purpose of one's work.

There should be a connection for everyone but if it isn't there among the leaders there will be a very steep hill to climb in creating a passionate and profitable purpose throughout the organization.

In no way do I have any intention of raising unnecessary doubts about purpose in your organization or life. Frankly if there really is purpose present, it will be unassailable no matter what I do. I could sweat and rant over you like a Tom Peters; probe with the gentle wisdom of a Peter Drucker; critique for the presence of greatness like a Jim Collins – and *nothing* would ever cause you to doubt your commitment to a meaningful purpose. True purpose can withstand any assault. There is no force greater on this earth than the power of purpose.

Here is my central point…

We don't know nearly as much about establishing an energizing, passionate and meaningful purpose as we think we do. The effort in some organizations is like hanging a "paint-by-number" painting in the Louvre. There may be breathtaking potential, unbelievable employee talent, a chance to set the industry on its head – and their statement of purpose has all the excitement and energy of an obituary.

It's not just about the passion – it's about the money. Purpose is profitable. Without it we throw sinful amounts of money away on abandoned projects and we leave untold revenue opportunities untouched. All totally preventable.

Believe it or not, there are people in the workplace who have a life-long commitment to being miserable and whiney. In fact they don't even like people who live passionately. They've never had a Happy Minute never mind a Happy Hour. This book isn't going to change that so to those folks I say, forget the passion – do it for the money.

Now let's push the leader's role in championing purpose a little further by taking a look at the first of the seven questions above as an example. And let's say your answer was a very quick "Yes, our executive team is unified and inspired by a common vision for this company." It's not that I don't trust your answer, but you know I couldn't let it go at that. I'd take each member of the team aside and ask them to briefly describe what that remarkable vision is. If I were to document each individual response and put them up on a PowerPoint slide, how much would you be willing to bet that, if it was your executive team, they'd all be the same?

I'll bet money that there would be major differences within your team and perhaps even out-right argument. You don't need me to apply this test – do it yourselves. If I'm wrong you truly deserve a celebration because you are indeed a purpose-driven organization and I enthusiastically congratulate you. On the other hand, if I'm right, we should talk.

I sat patiently listening to one senior group argue about whether or not they had a clearly defined vision. Finally I had to verbalize the obvious – if they had to discuss it – they didn't have it.

Having thrown my glove on the ground let me tell you where we're going with this purpose theme. First, we need a new language if we are to have new thinking so I will use the phrase *Peak Purpose*™.

This term refers to an organization's higher calling, a purpose that grips the heart and soul of all who work there and energizes them to peak performance and profitability. In other words we want to get as far away from the typical mission statement as we possibly can.

Every company, association, social service agency, school, sales team, project, department, division – *every* initiative you undertake – needs to define its peak purpose. It doesn't matter if it is a non-profit volunteer organization or the most lucrative money-making machine, you need a peak purpose.

Purpose statements that lead to both passionate performance and profitability share seven strategies that are not found in the typical "mission" or "vision" statement.

The first strategy is that a ***Peak Purpose is ecological***. This is all about defining why we are taking up space on this planet and how we relate to the rest of creation. I want to get you and your team thinking on a whole new level about purpose.

As I've gently suggested already, we know virtually nothing about the true power of purpose. What we all need personally and corporately is a higher purpose that will literally change the world for the better. The kind of purpose that will make you a legend in your industry.

The second strategy is to *let your irritations become your inspiration.* Here we explore where *purpose* actually comes from and you can be sure it is not a place most of us look.

Third, a **Peak Purpose** is *Awesome.* It will literally leave you awe struck. It will sound almost too grand and you will become nervous and feel the urge to do something mundane. This is why some people and organizations are literally afraid to have a highly defined peak purpose. This is a difficult chapter because no one is willing to admit to this universal and troubling problem. Sad too, because it is negating a great deal of profitable potential.

The Fourth Strategy of a **Peak Purpose** is that *it reflects the perspective of the customer or the people the organization serves.* Most statements of purpose are focused on what the organization wants for itself. Consequently the worse thing many companies could do is show their mission statement to their customers. It would drive them away faster than anything. The key thing here is to have your customers want you to be successful as much as you do. You won't believe the difference that makes.

Strategy Five is that a **Peak Purpose** is *written and expressed with passion*. I am always asked what a purpose statement should actually look like, and looking at how best to state or express a purpose results in a rather entertaining discussion. Should this be a dull and heavy tome in corporate-speak taking up the first four pages of a 30 pound personnel policy manual? Should it be more of a slogan that looks good on a T-shirt – or maybe something the employees can actually rap to? You'll find out in this chapter.

You can have a purpose statement worthy of Shakespeare but if you don't *communicate* it to those charged with fulfilling it you've wasted a lot of people's time. Strategy Six is that *a Peak Purpose is never out of sight*. Many companies, once they've grudgingly made it through their mission exercise, archive the document down in the basement with paintings of dead Chairmen, never to be seen again. This chapter says that keeping the purpose front and center is primarily the responsibility of leadership. If the team does not continually have their eyes on the goal posts you might as well hit the showers at half-time.

Strategy Seven is that a **Peak Purpose unites and energizes the organization in action**. This point will be a relief to those inclined to be task-driven, show-me-the-money types. Imagine sales united with service, head office with branch office, finance with IT, product line with product line, men with women – in short everyone united in a commitment to supernatural performance. A peak purpose must be fulfilled, the Universe demands it. Keep this principle in mind:

Peak Purpose always precedes peak performance.

What I am particularly eager for is an opportunity to explore the profitable power of purpose in your organization. I invite you to contact me without obligation. I'd enjoy talking with you.

With deep gratitude and joy I thank my wonderful wife Georgia, my dear friends Larry and Rose Mary Winget and Don Booty. Without their help, care and support fulfilling my purpose wouldn't be nearly as meaningful, or as much fun.

With my best wishes,

Ian Percy

1-877-502-3898
ian@IanPercy.com
www.IanPercy.com

The Profitable Power of Purpose.

STRATEGY #1: A Peak Purpose is Ecological.

I refuse to be drawn into a convoluted discussion about the difference between a "mission" and a "vision." The reason is I don't care.

Sitting around "defining our terms" is the most overused tool of procrastination in the corporate world today. By the time we define terminology one of two things could have happened: we could have finished the project in the same time period *or* the world has gone on without us and what we decide doesn't matter any more.

What I *do* care about is that you and your colleagues know who you are and what you are meant to do with your lives personally and corporately.

I believe most of our efforts to state a direction for ourselves or our companies are half-hearted at best. We sell ourselves so terribly short and are satisfied far too easily. I believe there is a *higher purpose* embedded in every human heart and in every organization we've created and it is our solemn duty to find and fulfill it.

Let me explain…

Purpose can be stated on two levels: an *economic* level or an *ecological* level. The term "economic" (the *oikos nomos* in Greek) refers to the rules and regulations in an organization; the things that might be called data and are easily measured. Sales numbers, cost per unit, market share – all qualify as items that fit well into an economic purpose. I'd have an economic purpose if I set out to write a bestselling 93-page book.

The term "ecological" (the *oikos logos*) is, to me, far more exciting. It literally means "the deep structure of the house" and begs to get at a reason for being that is deeper or higher or more meaningful or more visceral. This is what I mean when I use phrases like *higher purpose* or *peak purpose.*

I know that "ecological" is usually used in reference to salmon spawning grounds, ozone layers and recycling programs, but I'm inviting you to take a new spin on the word. This more ancient meaning is so wonderfully rich. It's the *logos,* the *Word*, the very meaning and beginning of existence. Applied here it refers to the most fundamental justification for your organization taking up space.

To stay with the book example, a more ecological purpose would be to write a book that prompts organizations to find their higher purpose and consequently make the world a much better place.

Do I write in order to make a boatload of money, or do I write because my spirit calls me to? If you were my personal coach, wouldn't you want me to say "Yes" to both?

But, after many years of speaking to and consulting with organizations of all types around the world, I've concluded that we excel in *economic* statements of purpose and are absolutely pathetic when it comes to *ecological* expressions. As will be discussed in Strategy Three, the idea of a higher purpose scares us half to death.

So yes, you need both economy and ecology in everything you do. However, my opinion is that, *before anything else*, you need an ecological statement of purpose. This is the purpose that makes whatever you are doing worth doing. This is what lights the fire in the belly and puts the sparkle in the eyes. This is what unites and inspires the entire organization to do something grand and transformative. This is like falling in love with your work and your work falling in love with you. You don't just have a purpose, the purpose has you.

Strategy #1 then, is to anticipate having a statement of your ecological purpose. At this point don't worry about what will actually be in that statement – it will come to you in time.

This is harder to do than you can imagine. What happens is that we write economic statements and pretend they're ecological. Some corporations don't even pretend. They are economic through and through. Their reason for living is to increase shareholder value. End of story.

There is sure nothing wrong with increasing shareholder value. I've got an investment portfolio too and lately I'd appreciate a little shareholder value.

The question should be: Is that your reason for living and working? If all you truly want is more margin and profit then you should have no compunction about hiring overseas workers to make your products for 50 cents an hour. Heck, it's 50 cents more than they were making isn't it? While you're at it, you can do quite well by linking to a few porn sites or maybe do one of those Nigerian "help me get $60 million out of the country" email campaigns. Getting into online gaming shouldn't be out of the question either.

When I push it to the absurd like that, most people will recoil. The recoil indicates that somewhere in their soul is at least a molecule of wanting to be associated with something of redeeming value. That molecule is all we need. We can nurture that seed into a market force of unbelievable purpose, passion and profitability.

Our problem is not one of motivation. We'd all like to leave a legacy of good while at the same time achieve prosperity. So why is this idea of an ecological purpose such an ordeal?

It's because we don't know ecological language on Wall Street. And it would be a rare professor who welcomes students into an MBA program by initiating a discussion of their divine higher purpose in life. Indeed, we get nervous in the presence of pure good and prefer to save it for the company Christmas party and the United Way campaign.

Am I advocating that goodness be a core operational strategy? Well, yes, that pretty well sums it up.

Which purpose would most likely stir the *souls* of a pharmaceutical sales team?

    a)   Our revenue target is $7.4 million in North American sales. Hit it and we'll take you to Cancun for three days.

b) This year we are going to help an additional 150,000 arthritis sufferers by showing them how they can live full and pain-free lives. To mark their victory as well as yours our sales team will meet in Cancun for a few days of celebration.

Do you see that both purposes involve the same sales activity? *But*...which one do you brag to your kids about? Can you imagine your kids saying, "Daddy, tell me again how you hit 115% of quota." Isn't the story of how you helped 150,000 people do more with their lives a better and more meaningful lesson?

Just semantics? Only to hard core economic cynics.

Defining a grand ecological purpose is a challenge for many organizations so I'll offer a relatively simple way of getting there.

Instead of jumping into some inane short-sighted and selfish rant about market share, ROI, being the biggest or baddest or No. 1, preferred supplier, low cost provider kind of thing, ask your-selves this question:

In what way(s) does our company want to make the world a better place through our service and/or products?

Do you make the world safer in some way?

Do you preserve beauty?

Are you helping to feed the hungry or house the homeless?

Are you arranging financial security for people?

How about curing some disease and bringing life-saving hope to desperate people?

Are you adding to human knowledge?

Do you bring joy and laughter into people's lives?

Have you found a way to feed animals so they are healthier?

Are you bringing ideas to life?

Do you make it possible for families to visit each other around the world?

Can you make digging holes less laborious?

To be even more blunt…

What good are you doing, exactly?

It is in this realm that you have a chance to find your inspired purpose. I'll tell you what, when you find that purpose you will know it! And you won't believe the impact it will have on you, your customers, your suppliers, everyone.

Is it possible for a company to find that they aren't doing any good in the world at all? I'm afraid so, but I don't have the time or space to go there. I'd prefer to assume that's not you.

Now for goodness sake, don't get into a discussion about how you are going to measure an ecological purpose. You will kill it if you do. You'll have enough things to measure in due time.

Every department, every project team, every unit needs an ecological reason for its existence if you want a positive energizing culture. This is not just an exercise because you need something for the "Our Mission and Values" link or to get some accrediting board off your back.

You also need economic statements of purpose, usually called goals. Here you satisfy your need to measure things. This is where you count your money. It is very likely you and your colleagues are brilliant at this so I'll not spend time on it here.

Think of a beautiful glowing fireplace on a white winter's night. The *fire* is your ecological purpose. This is what gives you the dream, spark, warmth, fascination, a meaningful reason to live and work. The *fireplace* is your economic measures. These give you safety, progress reports, tangible rewards, control. You need it all. The fire without the fireplace will burn your house down. The fireplace without a fire is a dull black hole.

The mistake you want to avoid at all costs is to obsessively focus on the economic level because you are feeling some kind of pressure to perform and deliver results. That will not lead to peak performance – only *peak purpose* leads to peak performance.

The most important thing I can tell you, and I tell you with absolute and total confidence, is that if you get your ecological or higher purpose right, the economic rewards will come to you. Try it the other way around and you will end up hopelessly busy, empty and meaningless.

The Profitable Power of Purpose

The Profitable Power of Purpose.

STRATEGY #2: Let your irritations inspire you.

If just reading the title for Strategy #2 doesn't throw you off, you are definitely headed for one majestic statement of purpose that will generate higher levels of meaningful work for your people and sustainable profitability for the company. Of that I am confident.

Purpose is, when you get right down to it, a *spiritual* force. Love is a spiritual force too. So is faith, forgiveness, service, generosity and all those "things" that make life not only bearable, but truly worth living. Just as an aside, I believe *leadership* is a spiritual force.

As I see it, meaningful work is a manifestation or a materialization of numerous spiritual forces coming together. And at the leading edge of these forces is *purpose*. It is the point on the arrow and without it you won't pierce the target. Instead you'll fall useless and pointless to the ground.

If after your weekend Mission and Vision Conference people do not talk about having had a spiritual experience – I respectfully suggest it was a failure. I don't doubt that you all came up with something but you simply cannot commit to a peak purpose without it being a spiritual experience.

I can just see the meeting room halfway through the exercise, walls covered in flipchart paper, key words and phrases circled in red, other words and phrases scribbled out and eliminated like some evil intruder had accidentally been given a marking pen. Everyone stood back and literally tried to read the handwriting on the wall.

The truth is some thing or some entity *was* trying to speak to you. It is the same universal force that gave Augustine, Mahatma Gandhi, Martin Luther King, Albert Einstein, Thomas Jefferson, Mother Teresa, Henry Ford, the Wright Brothers, Sam Walton, Howard Schultz, J. K. Rowling, Bill Gates, Oprah Winfrey, Michael Dell and Jeff Bezos their calling. What separates those who change the world from those who only exist in it is the ability to hear and respond to higher purpose.

There is absolutely no reason you and your

organization can't access this same power and all of the breathtaking treasures that go with it. I don't care if you're running a Mom and Pop Candy Store at the corner of Elm and Maple or a company about to break a billion in world-wide revenue – if you are not driven by higher purpose you don't matter.

How then does the "voice of purpose" speak to us?

You remember when your kids needed your help with a project and as you sat down to help them you said: "Okay, I'll get you started and then you'll have to finish it yourself." That is exactly what happened with creation. God (or the Universe depending on your belief system) started creation and then turned to us and said: "Now, you'll have to finish this yourself." Don't think Garden of Eden here, we trashed that a long time ago. Think down-town New York or Chicago or Los Angeles.

Completing creation isn't only about feeding the hungry in Ethiopia as important as that is. It is also about manufacturing car parts, food marketing, software development and retail sales.

The intention behind creating our existence is pure good. Our air and water are meant to be good. Our relationships and families all stem from goodness. Our work and our leadership are meant to be good. We are meant to be filled with peace and joy and prosperity on every level. In other words, the voice of purpose calls for what is universally good.

This is why the most important question from the previous chapter is: *What good are you doing, exactly?* Defining your organization's purpose is the same exercise as defining your organization's good.

You know you have found your good if the organization is filled with positive unstoppable energy; loyal appreciative customers; creativity and innovation; leaders that inspire just by walking down the hall; teams that revel in collaboration; sales professionals driven as much by cause as by commission, and a pervasive and confident knowing that you *must* do what you are doing. The reward is unimagined spiritual and material prosperity.

Sounds a little idyllic, doesn't it? Purpose *is* idyllic so we need to get used to it even if it does make us nervous. This doesn't mean life is challenge and trouble free. It means that when challenges rear their heads people see that as yet another opportunity to define even more sharply their higher purpose.

Organizations can know they are not *on purpose* when they are filled with irritations, restlessness, dissension, isolated silos, a tangled mess of ill-defined and costly projects, little evidence of leadership unity, desperate scrambles to re-brand, merge, re-structure, dismantle, etc.

The tragic mistake organizations make when faced with obstacles and confusion is that they fail to see it as a purpose issue. Instead they become even busier, create even more projects, re-engineer *again*, and scramble a little harder – like trying to put out a fire by throwing more wood on it. Instead, if they'd pursue the prosperity of *purpose*, they'd never have to deal with such futility again.

In the dark of my own past personal and professional turmoils I discovered an amazing pattern to our quest for meaning and higher purpose. It appears, to me at least, that the pattern applies equally to our personal lives and to our organizations.

If the pattern resonates with you, I encourage you read my book on leadership titled: *Going Deep: exploring spirituality in life and leadership* where it is described in considerably more detail. You will find it in the Inspiration Store at IanPercy.com.

INNOCENCE
The First Station

There are six "stations" to this pattern beginning with ***Innocence***. Every human enterprise starts off with a dream, a hope, a determination to do something wonderful. We believe that if you just work hard and participate with an honest heart good things will come to you.

Consequently we are shocked to learn that very

few people in this world really want us to succeed – and some of them actively lobby for our failure. You might call this being naïve. Colleagues with whom we shook hands to consummate a deal suddenly betray us without even a breath of hesitation.

INDEPENDENCE
The Second Station

With our first corporate wound we are ushered into the second station, *Independence*. Now we're mad. We will not be caught so foolishly again. In fact we turn all our energy into separating ourselves from those who threaten us or who have even the potential to threaten us. Our business is different. We offer better service, better workmanship, better value and we're open Sundays. In MBA school this is called branding. It is deciding how we want to appear to the world. It's all about differentiation.

Well guess what? There is still no guarantee of purpose here. The business is so busy defending its uniqueness it doesn't have the energy to actually go anywhere. A hockey team that focuses totally on defense and fails to score a goal can have no higher aspiration than a 0 – 0 tie. No one wins.

INSTITUTION
The Third Station

The business continues to grow. (You don't have to have purpose to grow, you just have to be lucky or be the only game in town.) Pretty soon you enter the labyrinth called **Institution**. To keep control and things organized you now need policies, procedures, rules. While once your entire company could fit in a van, you now have divisions and territories. It used to be that people did what had to be done without even thinking about it. Now you have job descriptions and span of control.

An "institution" is any human system where someone has the power to reward or punish people depending on how well they comply with the institution's rules. In many instances the situation has migrated from *free-for-all* to *fear-for-all*. Fit in. Don't rock the boat. Know your place. Do what gets measured. Hardly an environment conducive to higher purpose now is it? You'll get better results throwing flower seeds onto asphalt.

IRRITATION
The Fourth Station

Now here is where the magic begins to happen...

When people without purpose are in a work environment without purpose, they get restless. Really, really restless. Actually they get downright irritated – and that's why I call the fourth station **Irritation**. I'll spend some time here and then come back to tell you about the last two stations.

If you look at a factory or office tower full of people without a higher purpose for their own life working for a company without a higher purpose – just what do you expect? This is hardly a recipe for the good life.

The national epidemic is that people look for jobs, not for purpose. We should stop measuring the "job-less rate" and start measuring the "purpose-less rate." I can just hear it: "The purpose-less rate has risen to an all-time high of 95% according to the Labor Department."

Of course there is tremendous irritation in corporate America. It is the inescapable consequence of purposelessness. Our response, unfortunately, is to blame outsourcing to India, the Federal Reserve Board, or corporate corruption.

The only balm for irritation is clarity of purpose. So after a while, the absence of a higher purpose becomes a permanent spiritual condition and the irritation turns violent and destructive.

Chronically purposeless people then seek purpose in destruction, terrorism and suicide. And I am talking about *our* society, not al Qaeda.

So why is *Irritation* magical? Because purpose irritates us for our own good. A better way to put it is to say that purpose irritates us *toward* our own good. This is Destiny's voice calling us back to our higher purpose. If we listen to it, the rewards are enormous.

Why are we able to fly at the speed of sound to any point on the globe? Because the Wright brothers were irritated that they couldn't. Why do we have electricity? Because Edison got fed up working in the dark. Why will we find a cure for Cancer? Because a lot of irritated scientists are working on it. Why is Wal-Mart number one on Fortune's list? Because Sam Walton was irritated that common people couldn't get a good price on needed products.

And guess what – if your customers weren't irritated they wouldn't even be your customers! In fact they wouldn't need you any more than you need a mechanic while your car is running perfectly.

Consider this...

I don't know your company or its history. But I guarantee that it was started by someone who was irritated about something.

Go back to that original irritation. Why was your company started in the first place? Listen again to the voice that gave birth to your organization. What part of that original intent is still relevant today? If your company was founded in 1897, dress up in period costumes if you have to, but go back and experience your beginnings all over again.

Once you've done that, you've got to deal with today's irritations. The temptation is to try and drown any restlessness with typical institutional interventions like re-structuring, or merging or redesigning the corporate logo. Again, that would be like throwing fuel on the fire.

Listen to the voice. Move up close to the irritations and restlessness so you can hear better. Every angry customer is trying to help you. Every poor employee opinion survey is a message from God. Every percentage of loss in market share is a call from your higher purpose.

This exercise will help you do that. Try completing this sentence: *"Because* (identify the primary irritation you want to conquer) *we are committed to* (identify the solution you bring to this irritation).

I am not recommending that this be the actual statement of your peak purpose, but it will sure move you toward it. On the other hand if what you come up with grips your soul, run with it.

For example, an insurance company may state: "Because *too many hard working people are being financially ruined when hit with catastrophe,* we are committed to *providing them with superior financial resources and tools that will protect their financial future.*

A book publisher may conclude: "Because

25% of children are reaching adulthood without knowing how to read we are committed to *the production of books that entertain, engage and educate young students.*

An industrial coating manufacturer could say: "Because *many of the costly steel structures on which travel and business depend become seriously and prematurely eroded,* we are committed to *the research and development of coatings that dramatically and economically increase the lifespan of these structures.*

An orchestra might conclude: "Because *people need extra encouragement and inspiration in these days of uncertainty,* we are committed to *providing the most beautiful and uplifting music we possibly can through the channels people find most easily accessible.*

If you lead a supply chain improvement project your purpose might be: "Because *our customers are facing enormous economical pressure to control their inventory*, we are committed to *implementing a highly efficient and economical supply chain process that is compatible with all inventory software.*

In reading these examples don't you have a positive reaction to every one of them? You've never cared about industrial coatings but you read that example and you can't help but think: "Good idea, I hope you succeed." If you owned a steel bridge you'd call them this very second to learn about their product.

Basically you are saying: Here's something about the world that we don't think is right or that would make it a better place and here's what we are going to do about it. *That* is what makes work meaningful.

INSIGHT
The Fifth Station

There are two Stations left to mention. In forming your response to the current irritations with which you have been blessed, what you need is *Insight*. This is the fifth station.

Why are you experiencing these irritations? What do they mean? What can they teach you? Why did that project *really* fail? What is the voice trying to say? Irritations tell you to find a new way; to head in a new direction; to stop being driven by ego. Why look for "best practices" when you could be creating them? Seek wisdom instead of trying to win the debate. Ask your employees and customers what the irritations mean – they've known for some time and have been waiting for someone to ask.

When faced with the irritations you can go in only one of two directions: back into *Institution* where you will exacerbate the problem; or to *Insight* where you will be challenged to think and reflect more deeply, creatively and thoroughly than ever before. Take the road to Insight and you are on your way to the energizing and profitable power of your higher purpose.

INTEGRATION
The Sixth Station

If you allow the irritations to work their magic you will see everything come together – you will experience the confident strength of *Integration*. In this final Station of Integration, all initiatives make sense and all efforts are synergistic. There is no second guessing, no waste of time, energy and money. Decisions are wiser and faster because purpose is the supreme reference point.

Can you imagine sales integrated with service; finance integrated with IT; head office with branch; men with women; west coast with east coast; company with customer. Literally every dimension of your company will be in laser-like alignment, making the world a better place, doing the good you were always meant to do.

Remember that what you are seeking to define is your company's *higher purpose*, not some bland and safe corporate-speak that you can just rattle off. This peak purpose is revealed to you through what is irritating the organization, those in it and those it serves. Let your irritations be your guide.

The Profitable Power of Purpose

The Profitable Power of Purpose.

STRATEGY #3: Allow your purpose to be AWESOME.

One test for knowing you have found your organization's higher purpose is that you and your colleagues will literally be awe-struck with the grandeur and majesty of it. This experience is exhilarating and frightening at the same time.

To the ears of most organizations this concept will sound like an unintelligible lost language from some mysterious continent. It just doesn't compute. Not many people even faintly imagine that their job could have an awe-inspiring, grand and majestic outcome, never mind deliberately work toward making that true. There are people with count-down clocks on their desk telling them how much longer before they can retire, for Pete's sake!

Consequently this strategy will sound like an empty platitude if I don't set it up right so let me back up and make sure the foundation is in place. It is too important to take chances with it.

Strategy #1 was to set your expectations high – to be fully aware of the magnitude of this exercise. Think *high* and *deep,* not necessarily big. It is not a matter of knocking off some passable statement of mission, vision or frame of reference just so you can move on to the real work. The fact is that without a defined ecological higher purpose your work won't be real anyway.

Most examples of what are called missions and visions are bland, obvious, safe, unimaginative, soul-less, economically-oriented, cookie-cutter scripts. They make no difference whatsoever.

What did we all do before we had vision statements? Probably just what we are doing now. Not one single thing would change if the vision statement could somehow be yanked out of existence. Rarely in trying to decide where to allocate major capital funds, for example, does someone say; "Why don't we get out our vision statement and make sure we are allocating money *on purpose.*" In some places it would take an hour just to *find* the vision statement.

Now if that is not an accurate picture of what happens at your place, don't get annoyed at me for saying this. Be grateful that it doesn't apply to you.

But I've seen hundreds, if not thousands, of mission and vision statements and, believe me, it is a sad scene. It's like listening to the rejects of American Idol.

With a high expectation in mind, Strategy #2 directed you to look at what makes you and your organization restless and irritated. Circumstances containing the DNA of your higher purpose are happening to your organization every day. The trouble with most of us is that we don't know how to recognize destiny's voice.

Imagine having a 19-year old son with a tendency to drive too fast. He gets in an accident, totals his car and only by the grace of God is he still with you. Now what does he want to do? Get a faster car. Makes you mad just thinking about this situation doesn't it? Did he learn *anything* from this experience? How many more warnings will he be given before he will be no more? You just want to shake him and tell him to wake up and pay attention. "For your own *good* and for God's sake pay attention." we want to scream.

I don't even want to know how many times my consulting colleagues and I have tried to give warning messages to corporate clients. To us as outsiders the message was so obvious. If there were some way to do it, we'd love to make them wake up and pay attention. Why does it take a heart attack, an Enron collapse, a 9/11 to wake us, our companies and our country up to ask questions about what is important?

I wish I knew who it was who said: "To the blind all things are sudden."

Higher purpose comes out of *insight*, **not** from doing the same old institutional nonsense everyone else has been doing. Companies that become legends don't become legends because they followed somebody else's best practice. They get a grand and majestic picture of what they are uniquely meant to do. They go down the road less traveled. They make the world a better place – they find their own good.

Start talking about what restlessness gave birth to your organization in the first place. If the founder is still alive ask him or her to tell you about the moment they "heard the voice." If they've passed on, see if they wrote the story down anywhere. Then talk about what is making the organization restless now, both internally and externally. At every turn keep asking; "What does this mean?"

Each time you express your higher purpose something changes in the Universe. You'll not likely have an "Aha" for a while yet so don't worry about it. Most of the time we have to scrape away a lot of institutional rust before we get to the shiny metal.

What are we meant to do?
How do we want to make the world a better

place?

What good are we doing exactly?
What unique opportunity have we been given?
Would anyone miss us if we dissolved our
company tomorrow and, if they would, why would
they?

Ask these things over and over again. Chant them. Distribute questionnaires. Break into small groups. I don't care how you do it. Just start panning for the gold you know is there.

Here is the heart and reason for Strategy #3.

As you talk and explore, there will be the tendency to problem-solve and become institutional again. Don't allow it. If what is being expressed isn't inspiring, if it isn't making you sit up and take notice, if it isn't making you go "WOW"…you are off track. Look for *some-AWE* so your company becomes *AWE-some*.

Ready for something strange? Many people are afraid to be in the presence of the awesome. I'm talking scared to death. The word "awe" comes to us from Old Norwegian *agi* or "fright." It also contains the concepts of fear, anguish, pain, and grief. Not until the Bible was written was awe-fright combined with veneration, grandeur and majesty in reference to God, the Supreme Being. And not until the late 1900s did we start to use the word *awesome* to mean something "excellent."

Some of that old fear still lingers from our ancient heritage. But it need not. When God created the world, he declared it excellent and good. He declared it awesome. As we discover our good, and our organization's good, we too cannot help but declare it *awesome*.

Write out your peak purpose statement in a way that inspires. Stay away from corporate-speak. Don't be afraid of a few adjectives and a little drama, though you want to stop short of corny.

Remember a peak purpose is supposed to take your breath away. Every time you breathe you have one less breath left. Make it count. If something is going to take your breath away it should give you purpose and meaning in return.

The Profitable Power of Purpose.

STRATEGY #4: It reflects the perspective of the Customer or Client.

This point is a no-brainer but it is surprisingly hard to persuade bottom-line driven people about its bottom-line value.

Many mission, vision or purpose statements are greedy, selfish and self-centered. They often convey the impression that "we're going to milk as much money from our customers as we possibly can because our purpose is to become filthy rich at their expense." Luckily, most customers and clients will never see their supplier's mission statement which, in its current state, is likely a good thing.

If you walked into your doctor's office and

saw framed on the wall a notice that read: "My mission is to generate a million dollars in patient billings." – would your confidence and loyalty go up or down?

I'm sorry to tell you, but a lot of corporate mission statements have exactly the same impact. Phrases conveying that you want to be: "the largest, most profitable, dominating, preeminent, supreme, world leader with the largest market share" may sound like music to your Board and shareholders but they do absolutely nothing for those who can actually give you this result – your customers. Customers have enough struggles with their own bottom lines without having to worry about yours.

I've actually seen specific percentages enshrined in mission and vision statements. One included the phrase "to return to the shareholder 15% return on equity." Another included the goal of reaching the half billion dollar mark by a certain date.

Now can you *ever* imagine a customer gushing: "Oh how exciting – let's help them hit the half billion dollar mark by giving them our business."

Do you think your customers will value your service more because you can claim to be the "world's largest?" If you look at the world of management consulting, for example, being the biggest firm has actually become a detriment. It conveys inflexibility, pat cookie-cutter answers, unnecessarily expensive billing rates, high overhead, junior people doing the work and so on. Many companies today would rather work with smaller, highly competent and more personalized firms.

These days advertising that you want to be the biggest is like shooting yourself in the foot. Witness some of the backlash against Microsoft and Wal-Mart.

If your company or association has *anything* even remotely similar to this kind of language anywhere near your overall mission or vision, shred it, burn it, bury it, delete it, nuke it – whatever you have to do to keep it from ever seeing the light of day again.

The Principle of Reciprocity

Someone once said: "Help enough people get what they want and they'll help you get what you want." That is exactly the universal principle that applies here.

Put another way the principle is this: *When your peak purpose is also what your customers want, they will go out of their way to help you succeed.*

Your first question should be: "What do our customers want?" *not* "What do we want for ourselves?"

What is the benefit felt by the customers when you solve their problem(s) or bring an innovation to whatever it is they do? What would make them glad they hired you or bought your services and goods?

Take the language they'd use in their answer and, as much as possible, use it in forming your peak purpose statement.

Let's play with a few fictitious examples to drive the point home.

A University's mission statement could read: *To become the preeminent and most highly recognized education and research institution within the tri-state area.* Or it could be: *To help ambitious students decide what they really want to do with their lives and equip them to do it in a meaningful and rewarding way.*

Which one of those statements is most relevant to what your 17-year old daughter is going through as she thinks about what to do after high school? The first one is all about the university's ego, the status of its professors in the world of academia and their ambition to draw grants and donations to the school.

"What's wrong with that?" most people will ask. Absolutely nothing. Of course they want to raise money and of course they want the best, most talented faculty possible. But who is it they are serving and what do those "customers" want? If you research university mission statements, you will be shocked at how few actually focus on what the *student* needs and wants.

A company that repairs water damage could state: *Our mission is to employ the most advanced water extraction tools and techniques in providing water damage repair services to businesses and residences.* Or, as one such company actually puts it: *Like it never even happened.*

If I were sitting there, water up to my knees, my brand new HD television trying to breathe under water – which description would make me dial the number? There is no question…I just want all of this to go away.

A computer service company broadcasts: *We specialize in home office technology, providing hardware and software solutions including performance enhancement, security, virus protection, data backup, and networking capabilities.* This one seems straight forward enough and I really like the specific focus on home office technology, but it lacks two key concepts.

First, someone with a home office has likely committed his or her life to whatever it is they do and almost certainly have considerable passion around it. These people tend to associate with others who have passion. So where is the passion in the computer company's mission? There's none. That means they are probably boring, socially-inept geeks who speak a weird language.

Second, when am I most likely to need the service of a company that specializes in home office technology solutions? Probably about two seconds before I throw my computer through the plate glass window because I've lost my 79 page proposal because my stupid #*.&^%@ computer froze again!

So where is the urgency in this company's mission statement? There is none. They must think I'm just sitting around with nothing to do.

Might I not be reassured if their mission was something like: *We know what we're doing, we're fast, we know home office technology and we can save your sanity.* This, I suggest, has some personality to it and it responds to the essential burning questions of anyone needing the service.

The net of this discussion again is this: If you can declare an ultimate purpose for your company that draws as much excitement and passion from your customers as it does from your own people, you've got something very powerful. If it bores your employees, you are guaranteed it will bore your customers. And if it bores your customers you're better off not having a purpose statement at all.

Your customers are ready to help you achieve a level of success you can barely imagine...but first you have to help them accomplish their purpose.

Trust me, it is well worth the investment.

The Profitable Power of Purpose

The Profitable Power of Purpose.

STRATEGY #5: Express your passion.

"You've got to have an elevator speech." How many times have I been told that. Someone came up with this idea that we have only 30 seconds to tell our story and over time it became gospel.

We are told that any letter or proposal to an executive has to be on one page. Which angel brought that message down from heaven? The only reason your letter has to be short is if it's boring.

I do have to agree that if your speech or letter is all about you instead of about the benefits you can bring to the customer, the shorter it is the better!

Look…if an executive is in a showroom

looking at a metallic silver Porsche Carrera 4 Turbo, her absolute dream car – does she say to the salesperson, "Give me your elevator speech and the shortest brochure you've got." Of course not. She wants to hear the entire intricate story if it takes all day. She wants all of the brochures and the thicker they are the better. She wants to see pictures of a winding highway and a silver streak hugging the road. She wants to turn the page and see another picture just like it. Can't have too many pictures or too many details.

As an aside, a key part of the Porsche philosophy is to "convey the fact that emotion will always be a part of our vision." Shouldn't that be part of your vision too? Forgive me for I stray…but if you don't have any emotion in your vision then by all means keep it to 30 seconds.

At the other end of the spectrum are those who think a mission-type statement should include everything short of the color of the walls. One such resource suggests including customers, products, markets, technology, survival plans, philosophy, self-concept, public image and something about employees. Try getting all of that into 30 seconds.

This feels more like a strategic planning document or a position paper rather than an energizing statement of purpose.

All these components are important enough,

but I don't think they are part of declaring one's peak purpose.

But, regardless of my preferences, which way should it be if we really want to impact the passion and performance of other human beings? Is there an ideal "look" or format for a statement of purpose? Are there a minimum or maximum number of words you can use? Are there any rules?

In a word – no. Remember that your higher purpose is a *spiritual* force with which you are going to make the world a better place. You are expressing your corporate soul and you have no option but to express it *your* way. A true artist can do nothing else but express his or her art in alignment with who they are and the calling they've heard. The same applies to you.

Having said that, there are ways in which you can increase the likelihood that people will catch and be drawn to the passion and purpose that burns so deeply in your soul.

First a few things I suggest you *not* do:

1. **Do not include any terminology that deals with profit, shareholder value, market domination, margins, price, being the biggest, being #1 or anything with even a whiff of self-centered greed.** You may want to avoid terms like " sinfully profitable,"

"margins as wide as the Grand Canyon" or "cash cow."

As we saw in Strategy #4, you particularly want your customers and clients excited about your purpose and vision to the point where they actually *want* to help you achieve it. If they get the impression that you will do anything you can to grab every penny of revenue and profit *at their expense* they will wonder if you really care about their needs. If that happens, customer loyalty becomes very fragile.

2. **Don't make the history of the company your purpose statement.** Let me be clear...you should tell your story, just remember that a vision is about the *future*, not what has already happened.

Let's say your corporate story goes like this...

Incorporated just after WWII, Acme Nut & Bolt was founded by a young lanky 26 year old soldier who returned to Virginia to find his farm equipment in disrepair. Frustrated by the scarcity of the simple nuts and bolts he needed to hold his disintegrating equipment together, he sought the help of his neighbor; an old-time blacksmith nicknamed Cranky Charlie...

Even though I made this story up, I'd like to

know how it turned out. This sounds like a good story. Indeed, some companies have stories worthy of Hollywood. They bring tears to your eyes and new courage to your soul and they need to be told over and over again.

My point is: don't tell it under the heading of a vision, mission or purpose statement. Why ruin a perfectly good story by calling it "Our Mission?" It's *not* a mission.

Call it "Our Story" or "The Birth of Our Vision." Come up with something dramatic like: "A Legacy of Passion" or "Our Inspired Past – Our Confident Future" or "Our Past Energizes Our Future." How about: "Some passions get stronger over time – how our yesterday inspires our tomorrow." And then by all means under headings like those, tell us how the company came to be and how it got to this place. The point to remember here is that your actual vision or purpose statement is about the *future*.

3. **Don't tell us what you are currently and obviously doing.** A residential real estate company notes as their Mission: *"We sell houses."* Now doesn't that make the hair on your arms stand up. And what a great way to distinguish this real estate company from all others!

An accounting firm writes: *"Our mission is to provide comprehensive accounting and financial services including but not limited to tax preparation, budgeting, investment advice and payroll services."* Again – this doesn't exactly make me wish there was a job opening. Can you imagine anyone saying "I've dreamt about doing this my whole life."

Some of my best friends are in real estate and accounting but even they would have to admit that there isn't one iota of vision or emotion in this approach. No appeal to anyone whatsoever.

4. **Don't be lazy.** Far too often organizations can't be bothered to find their higher purpose choosing instead to set the bar at the lowest level they possibly can and still make payroll. These are the ones who limp through life, hire unexciting people to do unexciting work, whine and groan about evil government forces and on and on. They are pathetic and I don't want to give them my business.

The "mission" I've seen a thousand times from these types if I've seen it once is: *"Our mission is to become the preferred supplier in our chosen marketplace."* How many meetings did that one take? They actually frame it and hang it on a wall. It's a sad reflection of a sad company.

I've got news for these people – customers *always* go to their preferred supplier. If you aren't a preferred supplier, you don't even get to play the game never mind win it. It would be more honest to put up a sign that says, *"Our mission is to scrape by."*

What you *should* think about in declaring your higher purpose.

1. **Write it in a way that is appealing to your customer.** I don't apologize for the redundancy of this point – it is just too important. Don't ever, ever, ever write a branding document you wouldn't want your customer to see. If your purpose doesn't appeal to the people you want to attract – then exactly what is it you are trying to do?

2. **Create a long *and* a short version.** I believe that if you have a story to tell, you should tell it. Why some companies knock off their whole purpose in a single sentence or paragraph is beyond me. Maybe it's because there's no passion behind it. But if you *are* passionate, surely the very reason for your existence deserves more than a line or two.

   So by all means write a page, several pages, or a small book about your purpose, where it comes from, what it means to you, how it will make a difference to people and companies.

Now here is the trick to doing this…

Don't have your typical PR person write it. In fact don't have anyone who isn't a full-blown writer do it. There will be just too much corporate spin-'n-speak. Find someone who has written a Harlequin Romance novel, an ex-National Enquirer columnist, or someone who writes infomercial copy to do it. This copy has to sing. It has to convey the *passion* you feel about your purpose. You want people to say, "I couldn't put it down."

This document is what you use to educate new employees and customers. This explains what you are all about. It should become your major marketing tool so put considerable creativity, time and money into it. Be proud of it.

Once the vision takes root in the minds, hearts and souls of your people, then, *and only then*, should you start working on the "catchy" version. Unfortunately this is where most organizations start. If the vision isn't already alive and well, creating something cute and clever will actually mitigate the vision, not help it.

Coming up with a mantra, a phrase or slogan that would look good on a golf shirt is a terrific idea. Imagine getting it down to a single word and when that word is uttered it expands to fill the hearts and minds of employees and customers alike with the grand, full and rich reason your company exists and how you are making the world a better place.

I had that very experience when I was in Bahrain teaching a week-long program on advanced leadership to about 90 Saudi Arabian corporate presidents. They all worked for one huge conglomerate. We were talking about mission and purpose. I had no sooner introduced the topic when people were murmuring something. "What is it?" I asked, hoping I hadn't offended in some way. "Aamar al ard" they said in a tone of real passion and reverence. "What is that?" I enquired. They said that was their collective purpose and vision. I pressed for an explanation. "It means contributing to the development of the earth and the welfare and prosperity of the whole community."

All that in one word embracing the whole peak purpose of their existence. I loved it.

Get *that* to happen, and people will wear the golf shirt proudly.

The Profitable Power of Purpose

The Profitable Power of Purpose.

STRATEGY #6: Keep the purpose flag flying high.

Walk into a randomly selected business, stop the first employee you see and ask him or her to tell you what the mission or peak purpose of their company is. A more brutal way to pose the same question is to ask why they are spending so much of their non-renewable time – time they will never get back – working for this company.

Get fanciful and picture this for a second: that person stops dead in their tracks and their eyes get misty as they motion for you to sit down for a moment. After a couple of deep breaths to collect themselves they begin to tell you with obvious pride and gratitude about the grand purpose of their company and how they are part of a team wholly committed to making the world a much better place. You thank them and get up to leave but they pull you back down saying, "Wait, there's so much more." Politely you listen as they describe the meaning of their own work and how blessed they feel just to be part of this higher purpose.

Now if that happens in *your* organization, you can put this book down without finishing it because you don't need it. Even better, give it to someone in another company who does. As corny as that description may sound, it is *exactly* the kind of reaction we're after. You've got to admit, it's a long, long way from the probable and dumbfounded "What mission?" response you'd get in many organizations.

There are executives who think the whole purpose thing is nonsense and if everyone would just do their job properly everything would be fine. These are the same executives who claim; "I don't care if people like me as long as they respect me." But that's another whole problem. We don't have to concern ourselves with these people because they aren't reading this anyway.

The truth is that most companies have at least a token mission or purpose statement. Apart from the quality of it, why don't typical mission statements have much impact?

My observation is that, even with the most

passionate, awesome and customer-oriented peak purpose there is usually only a token launch of what should be the most dramatic and vital tool in the company's competitive strategy. Instead it fizzles on the launch pad with the explanation: "Well we sent an email around and put it on the website." Or, "We give a copy to new employees on the first day of orientation." With that kind of minimalist introduction is it any wonder the mission disappears into the nether land?

If a company was launching a new product, would they take out one ad to introduce it? Of course not. Your advertising people know a new product won't even appear on the consumer's radar screen until they've been hit over the head with it a couple of dozen times. Exactly the same process is needed in launching awareness of a peak purpose and having it embedded in the hearts and minds of your employees and customers.

For a peak purpose to make a significant impact on the performance and profitability of the organization it has to be virtually omnipresent – literally everywhere all at once.

First write it on the heart

More important than having your purpose engraved in marble or framed on the boardroom wall, is having it written on the hearts and souls of those whose responsibility it is to fulfill it. Look at people scurrying about the warehouse and you see peak purpose. Follow one of the sales guys on his calls and you see peak purpose. Watch the maintenance man figure out why there's no hot water in the rest room and you see peak purpose. Witness senior executives negotiate the purchase of a smaller company and you again see peak purpose. It is through manifestations like these that you know your purpose lives and has taken deep root. This is the most important evidence of all.

With this foundation and the assurance that your purpose has a life of its own, make it *the* reference point for everything that happens. Here are a few suggestions.

Make it part of the hiring process

Far too often the hiring process and the subsequent orientation week are entirely forgettable experiences. It is not enough to note the purpose statement on page six of the employee manual right before the section on employee benefit policies.

So how about in the hiring interview you simply hand them a copy of the company's peak purpose and ask them to circle what they think are the key words. Then have them talk about what each word conveys to them and how they could see themselves making that word real on the job. For example, say they circle the word "service" in the purpose statement. What do they really mean by that, since the word is bandied about by lots of organizations who barely know how to spell it? How would they describe "acceptable service" compared to "exemplary service?" Ask them how they've been served even in the recruitment and hiring process. That'd be a telling conversation, now wouldn't it?

Do you ever ask potential employees what the peak purpose of their life is – and what that purpose has to do with the job they are applying for? I guarantee if they don't have a clear direction for themselves, it won't matter much what corporate purpose you put in front of them. Relating personal purpose or destiny to the purpose of work is without doubt the primary focus of my thinking, speaking and writing. And it is a dimension almost totally overlooked in the corporate world.

Also in the orientation experience spend time telling the corporate story. Why and how was the company created? Who have been the key personalities and the driving forces for change and innovation? Let them meet some of these people so they catch their spirit and dream.

If you have a mission mantra, an easily remembered phrase that summarizes your peak purpose, have them memorize it right there and give them the embroidered golf shirt for doing so.

Make it the heart and standard of your education and training programs

Deeply analyze your peak purpose identifying all the behaviors and skills that will be needed to make it live and breathe every minute of every day. Use those components as the organizing structure for all education and training programs.

You no longer buy just a convenient change management or leadership program off the shelf because somebody recommended it to you – you find the program most in alignment with your peak purpose.

If I know anything I know training and development and believe me there is huge disparity in the philosophy and principles on which education programs are created. "Leadership" is the best example. In no other subject area will you find greater differences between programs. You need to be sure what you select exemplifies your peak purpose and your principles.

Make it part of your performance improvement process

I'm not a believer in "performance review" but I am a huge fan of "performance improvement." Instead of the usual standard stuff that shows up on performance evaluation forms, all you need is the purpose statement. The discussion opens like this: "Let's look at all the ways in which your performance has helped fulfill our peak purpose and made the world a better place and then we'll talk about how you can eclipse even that level of performance over this next year."

Write it everywhere

And I mean everywhere. Obviously it should be on every office wall, in every meeting room, in the cafeteria, in the elevator – everywhere.

Print it on the tent cards used in the seminars and workshops. Print it on employee checks if you still use those. Print it on paper place mats in the cafeteria. If it is a powerful purpose statement that people actually believe in, you just can't over do it...unless you insist on employee tattoos.

Make it a symbol of achievement

If you can, turn your peak purpose into a symbol. The Nike swoosh is the most commonly cited example. The symbol could be something recognizable like a flame or chain links. Or it could be an abstract expression to which people apply meaning. Something like this can then be produced in lead crystal or stainless steel and given as a award to those who perform supernaturally. Make it the "Peak Purpose Performance Prize."

Have it as the "hook" in every marketing and PR initiative.

If the peak purpose is real, alive and written

well, it will draw customers and clients to you like bees to honey. Don't put it below the fold in 9pt. font right next to the disclaimer paragraph. Your purpose is the most powerful tool in your marketing and public relations arsenal, so use it.

Have you noticed Daimler Chrysler ads lately? Their mission is to make cars interesting and cool again. Innovate. Innovate. Innovate. And what phrase do you see in every ad? "Innovation comes standard."

We are not talking a slap happy slogan here, let's get clear about that. What we are looking for is a succinct way of expressing a living, breathing, awe-inspiring peak purpose. Thrill the customer with your purpose and they'll thrill you with profitability.

Make the peak purpose the most repeated statement heard from every executive.

Finally, no executive should *ever* give a presentation to employees or to customers without passionately referencing the peak purpose of the company. They don't have to do it at their daughter's wedding, but they should have thought about it.

You may have seen the television commercial where at a wedding reception a guy is talking with pride and emotion about the bride, how she had grown through the years and his wishes for a happy and secure future for this wonderful couple. Suddenly he stops and says, "Well I'm just their financial advisor, let's hear from her dad." That's what I'm talking about!

There's an old Christmas carol that starts with "Go tell it on the mountain, over the hills and everywhere!" If you have good news about what your company is doing to bring safety, beauty, health, prosperity, education, laughter or peace to the world, please...*go tell it on the mountain!*

The Profitable Power of Purpose

The Profitable Power of Purpose.

STRATEGY #7: It unites and energizes the organization into action.

If the team motto at your place is "Every man for himself." then you need a unifying and energizing peak purpose more than you know.

Even large and sophisticated companies tend to work in silos and at times the various departments or divisions actually work against each other. Apart from the personal stress and strain of working in an environment like that, maintaining an internally competitive culture is just plain costly. How can these companies afford this waste and the abuse it heaps on customers? Do they not have enough competition and problems from external factors? I don't get it.

Part of the problem is that aggressive managers (I won't call them leaders) like to have a clearly defined territory they can command and control. For example, in no way is Service about to let Sales tell them how to do their job. After all, we know sales-people are out there golfing, having a two hour lunch, driving their fancy company cars. All they care about is winning the Chairman's Circle trip to Bali. When's the last time Service people had a trip – to Boise, never mind Bali?

We could look at IT and Finance as an uneasy alliance as well. Techies speak a language no one else understands and represent an insatiable money hole. Finance bean counters want "an accounting" of where these millions of dollars are going and want to know the ROI. IT is trying to get the company on the leading edge, while Finance is trying to control and perhaps restrict expenditures.

The challenge for leaders dealing with these examples as well as all the other natural food-chain predators, is to find a way to actually unite them so the whole becomes greater than the sum of the parts. It turns out there are only two ways to do it.

There is one way we've seen employed throughout history over and over again – and I say that sadly. That way is: "If you want to unite the country, go to war." And it works, at least until the war is over and then it's every man for himself again. A threatening force could unite your company too, such as when everyone unites to thwart a hostile takeover or a pending bankruptcy. Again, once the threat is over, so is all the supposed unity. A negative force cannot sustain unity or performance.

Major re-engineering or re-organizational initiatives don't qualify as unifiers, not even temporarily. They tend to force people into self-preservation mode.

What you need is a force that will unify the troops in sustainable supernatural performance no matter what happens in the marketplace. My suggestion will not be a shock to you...*if you want to unify your company in sustainable and profitable performance, find and promote a meaningful peak purpose that creates good in the world.*

Instead of going to war, go to purpose.

Only a higher purpose is powerful enough to overcome the need to command and control. Only a higher purpose can cause people to put the good of the whole above their own needs and wants. It is *purpose* that compels people to do the very best job they can and to look for new ways to thrill clients and customers. Frankly, purpose is the most powerful force on earth and probably the most under-used, certainly in the corporate world.

A true peak purpose like we have been discussing all through this book cannot help but unify and energize your people. That's a fact.

What if your purpose doesn't peak?

So what if after you've poured your soul into identifying and communicating what you consider to be a high and noble purpose, you don't see any evidence of greater unity or performance? What if after all this you see people roll their eyes, nod politely and go back to just doing a job?

One of two things has to be your conclusion. The first is that there is still work to do on defining your peak purpose. Somehow you haven't quite put your finger on it in a way that releases its latent power.

Maybe something was missing in how you went about it. If the President went away to his or her hunting lodge for the weekend and came back announcing a new "vision" on Monday morning, then no wonder no one is excited about it. You don't need to make this a multi-year project by having absolutely everyone involved in every aspect of the discussion, but there does need to be participation so ownership is ensured. There are lots of ways to do this effectively and efficiently but it depends on the specific situation. Remember this: *When people plan the battle, they don't battle the plan.*

Maybe it is how it was being expressed. Anyone who writes direct marketing copy will tell you that changing just one word in an ad can increase the response rate several hundred percent. Words are the mystical connection between us all and the trick is to find the ones that trigger an emotional and spiritual response. The purpose itself has to be your own, but get help with your wording. I want to stress again, however, that the exercise is not a copywriting one – it is a purposeful one. Don't let some cute, clever slogan take precedence over substance.

I mentioned there are two potential reasons a purpose doesn't peak. The second is that you have too many of the wrong people working in your organization. Some people have no meaning or purpose for their own lives and, as I've noted already, those people won't get excited if you've figured out a way to solve world hunger. *Nothing* will excite them.

Other people may have a clear personal purpose but it has nothing to do with the work they are doing. At least these people understand "purpose." What they need to do is find a connection between the corporate purpose and their life purpose. If they can't, then they need to find a work outlet where there is one.

You want your place filled with people who have a personal sense of destiny and who see working in your company as a way of fulfilling that calling.

This thought is not in the scope of this book, but companies need to start incorporating evidence of personal purpose into the hiring and promotion processes. If a company is filled with purpose-full people they will lead their competitive field, no question about it. Nothing is more powerful than the purpose-driven organization.

Making the whole greater than the sum of the parts

When the most important force in the company is the fulfillment of purpose, you know it's working.

I've seen companies use the corporate purpose as the ultimate reference point in the annual budgeting process in a way that would bring tears to your eyes. Each department tells the other departments how it plans to fulfill the peak purpose and what financial support it needs to do so. It is the other departments that say "Yes" or "No" to that request based on how well the plan fits the purpose.

Sometimes they will suggest a joint plan between two or more departments because the ideas overlap. Sometimes I've heard a department head say "What you want to do is more important than our project and we'll withdraw ours so the money is available to you."

This is night and day compared to the usual strategy of padding your budget because it's going to be cut back anyway or trying to position your plan as much more important than that of another department in "dog eat dog" style. In this case, departments aren't adversarial because the overriding interest is to do the thing that will fulfill the peak purpose in the most effective and efficient way. *Whatever it takes for the good of the whole* is the rule, not *what's good for me is good for you.*

I've had clients implement a departmental or divisional performance improvement process. Respective leaders get together to discuss what further contributions each group could be making to fulfilling the corporate purpose. One major hospital used to have an annual "Review and Rejoice Rally" where department leaders would not only seek support for new ambitious plans, but would recognize and thank each other for the support they had received during the previous year.

Nothing is more beautiful than a purpose-driven organization fully intent on making the world a better place. Nothing is more meaningful and nothing is more profitable. The good *do* win!

Sometimes we equate strong margins, competitive leadership, dominant market share and enviable profitability with unfeeling, workaholic, stress-laden, hard-driving, lean and mean organizational culture. And I'll admit you can make money that way. If that is all you want out of life then go for it. But if you want to make a meaningful contribution to this world *and* enjoy the material rewards that go along with it...*the power of a peak purpose will take you there.*

The Profitable Power of Purpose.

The Strategies Summarized

Strategy #1 A Peak Purpose is Ecological.

Strategy #2 Let Your Irritations Inspire You.

Strategy #3 Allow Your Purpose to be AWESOME.

Strategy #4 It Reflects the Perspective of the Customer or Client.

Strategy #5 Express Your Passion.

Strategy #6 Keep the Purpose Flag Flying High.

Strategy #7 It Unites and Energizes the Organization Into Action.

The Profitable Power of Purpose.

If you want to stir up animated discussion about your organization's *Peak Purpose™*...

Ask these 20 Wicked Questions.

1. What percentage of our employees are able to accurately describe the overall mission, vision or purpose of our organization?

2. How well known is the story behind our mission or vision?

3. Is our statement of overall purpose economical or ecological?

4. Have we let our experiences, irritations and thoughtful intuition influence our statement of purpose?

5. Is there a sense of reverent awe when we read or hear our Peak Purpose?

6. Does our Peak Purpose reflect the perspective of our customers or clients or is it just about what we want for ourselves?

7. When an objective person reads or hears our mission/vision, do they catch the degree of passion we have for it?

8. Are we as an organization actually and truly passionate about our purpose?

9. Is there evidence of our Peak Purpose every where you look in our organization?

10. Do we know beyond a doubt that our Peak Purpose burns even more brightly in the hearts of our executive leaders?

11. Has our mission or vision been a significant factor in unifying and aligning our entire organization structure, operations and culture?

12. How well do our customers and clients know and support our ultimate purpose?

13. Is there concrete and ongoing evidence that our work is truly making the world a better place?

14. In our organization do we ever talk about how a personal sense of purpose needs to relate to the corporate purpose?

15. Do we take significant time at the outset of every project and initiative to define a Peak Purpose?

16. Have we ever had people want to work with us specifically because they identify strongly with our mission?

17. Do we hold each other accountable for our contribution to the fulfillment of our Peak Purpose?

18. Are we ready to do what it takes to fulfill our purpose or do we tend to cling to old patterns and behaviors?

19. Have we ever said "No" to a major opportunity because it didn't fit with our purpose?

20. When some day we look back at our service to this organization, will we proudly know beyond a doubt that our lives and our work have been purpose-full and that we have left a legacy of enduring value?

The Profitable Power of Purpose

About Ian Percy

Almost every speech he gives, every hour he consults and every word he writes is about finding *Peak Purpose*™ and releasing this incredible power to make the world a better place.

Ian Percy has been declared "One of the top 21 speakers for the 21st century" by *Successful Meetings* magazine. He is one of only three speakers in the world inducted into *both* the International and Canadian Speaking Halls of Fame.

A registered organizational psychologist, Ian is internationally acclaimed for his remarkable ability to blend depth of insight, inspiration and unending humor in helping organizations and individuals rise to higher levels of purpose, passion, performance and profitability.

His clients include the likes of Microsoft, Transamerica and Exxon Mobil. Ian speaks with equal ease and impact to scientists, sales people, financial specialists and the technologically inclined – to groups of ten or ten thousand.

A respected author, Ian has written six books some of which have been translated into several languages. He is also a columnist on performance improvement for *Human Capital* magazine read by over 40,000 HR leaders.

A Canadian, Ian and his wife Georgia now live in Scottsdale, Arizona with their white labrador *Destiny*. They have an active interest in reining Quarter Horses and get in the occasional game of golf.

www.IanPercy.com

Other Purpose-full Resources

**These inspirational products are available from
www.IanPercy.com**

Going Deep: exploring spirituality in life and leadership

This is Ian's breakthrough book on leadership. Available as a Soft Cover Book and as an 8 CD Audio album

The 7 Secrets to a Life of Meaning

THE book for anyone wanting to find their purpose in life! Also available as a 6 CD Audio Album.

The 11 Commandments for an Enthusiastic Team: collaborating with purpose and passion.

*If you lead a team, any team, you need this book! Comes as a Gift Set with book **and** CD in an attractive embossed sleeve.*

The 11 Commandments video and posters

This inspirational team building video is being used around the world! Ask about the frameable 11 Commandments personal posters. also available in conference room size.

1 Question 2 Answers

Ian Percy and Larry Winget answer vital questions about life...because sometimes you need gentle spiritual guidance and sometimes...a swift kick in the butt!

Substantial discounts offered on quantity purchases

**www.IanPercy.com
1-877-502-3898**